To James, from
Aunt Rita.

Welcome aboard my little
book, this 90th. year since
the sinking of 'Titanic'.

John Hodges.

April 14th., 2002.

TITANIC

John Hodges

VANTAGE PRESS
New York

For Nick—a very special person—1979–1998

This is a work of fiction. All names and places have been changed, and any similarity between the names, characters, and places in this book and any persons living or dead is purely coincidental.

FIRST EDITION

All rights reserved, including the right of
reproduction in whole or in part in any form.

Copyright © 1999 by John Hodges

Published by Vantage Press, Inc.
516 West 34th Street, New York, New York 10001

Manufactured in the United States of America
ISBN: 0-533-12927-3

Library of Congress Catalog Card No.: 98-90815

0 9 8 7 6 5 4 3 2

Contents

Foreword   v
About the Author   vii
Prologue   ix

One.	The Competition	1
Two.	The Tour of *Titanic*	7
Three.	The Stowaway	21
Four.	Cherbourg and Ireland	26
Five.	Out into the Atlantic	35
Six.	That Fateful Night	41
Seven.	Women and Children First	46
Eight.	The Final Plunge	52
Nine.	Rescue by the *Carpathia*	60
Ten.	New York	64

Foreword

Ellen Mary Walker—*Titanic*
I have been asked to write a foreword for John, and accepted with pleasure. We both share a fascination and interest for *Titanic* and of course I have a very personal interest because my parents were on board.

My father was Henry Samuel Morley, who owned confectionery shops in both Worcester and Malvern. My father was forty years of age and a millionaire when he decided to leave his wife and daughter and start a new life in California with Kate Florence Phillips, the pretty nineteen-year-old assistant from his shop near the railway station in Worcester.

Leaving provision for his wife and daughter, Henry and my mother, Kate, registered on Titanic in the assumed names of "Mr. and Mrs. Marshall." My father, Henry Morley, went down with the "unsinkable" *Titanic*, but Kate was bundled aboard the last lifeboat to leave the stricken vessel.

The disaster was on April 15, 1912, with myself being born on January 11, 1913, at the home of my grandparents in Waterworks Road, Worcester, just nine months later.

Among my most prized possessions is a poignant reminder of *Titanic*, my mother's purse which she carried on the ship, still with her cabin keys inside!

I hope you enjoy this version of the *Titanic* story, which I have read and helped with as an advisor.

Ellen Mary Walker—October 1998

E M Walker

About the Author

John Hodges is an Englishman who lives in Worcester, an ancient, beautiful city close to the border with Wales. Mr. Hodges was educated at Bedstone College, a private boarding school sited in a magnificent reproduction Tudor mansion on the Shropshire border. After leaving school, he worked and lived on his father's stock and arable farm near the Roman city of Wroxeter in Shropshire before moving to London, where he was employed by the Collins Publishing House.

After attending Christ's College of Education in Liverpool and gaining his degree in Education and an Advanced Special Needs Diploma, Mr. Hodges first taught in a Junior School for a period of twelve years before moving on to Cruckton Hall, near Shrewsbury, as a teacher for boys with "behaviour and learning special needs." He spent some months teaching English at a private school in Jeddah, Saudi Arabia, before taking up a post at Sunfield School, Clent, in the West Midlands, where he taught children with "severe learning disabilities" for three years.

Mr. Hodges currently works as a part-time teacher and writer in Worcester, England.

Prologue

The gigantic liner moved gracefully through the silent, calm sea, the waters strangely smooth, a mirror of the star-studded sky above, as if at that moment all eternity appeared to be still and at peace.

In the magnificent staterooms on board, first-class passengers were enjoying themselves, dancing and dining as the sound of lively ragtime filled the cold night with sound.

The silent menace far out in the ocean moved closer on its collision course; it was probably not a colossus—perhaps only about one hundred feet in height, but deadly. When the giant ship was struck, the impact felt like little more than a shudder to those on board.

That small, almost imperceptible shudder had caused a wound from which she would never recover; it was a mortal blow that would mean, in just less than two hours, the ending of the short life of one of the largest and finest ocean liners ever built.

In that short space of time, there were experienced great moments of courage and great fear, for everyone knew there were not enough lifeboats for all on board.

As she dipped further by the bow into the cold, unmerciful sea, she seemed to almost stand on end for a few moments as if in prayer, before plunging two miles to the ocean floor, her passing marked with only a swirl of cold, white foam, piles of flotsam, and the cry of many hundreds of people who were soon to drown in the freezing cold waters of the North Atlantic Ocean.

One
The Competition

I remembered that fateful morning as if it were only yesterday. It was the day I was to receive the result of the competition, and a day that was to change the rest of my life in a way that I could never have imagined.

That particular day started in the Children's Home just like any other. The matron had rung the bell at 7:15 A.M. sharp for all the children to be up, washed, and dressed before the bell for breakfast at 7:55 A.M.

The home was run like any typical English boarding school, with a strict timetable that covered every part of the day. The only time the guardians did not make time for, was time to talk to each of us individually. They were never unkind and cared for us all very well, but we were never special.

It had been four years now, almost to the day, that both my parents had died while on the continent on holiday. They had been involved in a horrific train crash close to Paris. After their sudden deaths, there were no relations or friends who were prepared to take in an orphaned teenage boy. So the local authorities had no choice but to take me away from the fee-paying prep school that I had been attending and place me in a childrens' home.

At the time, after the initial shock of losing my parents and my home, I felt the home was in fact better than the school. There was no more bullying or fagging, but I missed my family life very much indeed and it took a long time to adjust to the changes that had suddenly and cruelly altered my life. It was many months before I stopped looking out of the window on a Saturday or Sunday morning expecting my parents to turn up laughing and smiling to take me out for the day as they had done at school.

I suppose it was this idea of getting away from the home for a few hours into the real world that first started me to be interested in having my own bicycle, and so a chance to escape for a while. The boys were allowed to go for a walk or a ride on weekends, as the home was situated deep in the Shropshire countryside, with few fears for our safety.

I forget now where I first saw the competition mentioned; it may have been the local newspaper or in the multitude of magazines that always littered the library, left by some well-wisher or visitor. What caught my eye when I saw the detail was in fact the second prize, which was a new bicycle. The first prize had hardly any interest for me, something to do with a visit and tour of one of the new White Star liners that had just been launched in Belfast.

To enter the competition, you had to write a short story. I decided to write a ghost story, not because I thought I was any good at writing, but every evening one of the boys or a member of the staff had the habit of telling a story before the lights went out, the more ghastly and frightening the story the better. So, after four years, I had quite a few stories to tell. I decided to use and alter one of the stories I had heard. I wrote it out and sent it off, believing that I had little chance of winning, but still hoped.

It must have been about a fortnight later, at breakfast, that the matron brought round the mail, which was always handed out at this time of the day. Having no-one who really cared about me out in the world, I had very few letters, so when she handed me a large brown envelope addressed to a Mr. Edward Eastcliffe, I was most excited. I tore open the envelope, with the rest of the table looking on with curious eyes, and pulled out the contents. It was a single sheaf of paper stating that I was the winner of the competition and offering their congratulations.

A friend who was sitting next to me grabbed the letter and shouted, "It's Edward—he won a competition. It is a visit and tour of R.M.S. *Titanic!*" Everyone cheered and offered me their congratulations, but I did not feel the same excitement. Who wanted to look around a boring ship? I had never been to the sea and would probably be sick in the harbour. What I really had hoped for was the bicycle, a dream now lost, for what chance would I have now? I even thought of writing to the organisers to ask if I could change the prize, but I knew they would not do that. I decided to look at the good side, which I supposed was a chance to have a whole day out on my own, something I had not been allowed to do since I came to live at the home more than four years ago.

As the news of my win spread, the rest of the children and the staff became quite excited, although I did not feel the same joy. In fact, overnight I became somewhat of a celebrity. Even Raymond, the "egghead" of the home, spoke to me. He rarely spoke to anyone. He was always in the library or sitting somewhere with an open book on his lap. Every time now he passed me or saw me, he would make the point of giving me some new fact about the ship. "Do you know she is said to be 'unsinkable'?" he said. "They say that even God himself could not sink that ship. She is the largest and safest passenger liner ever built!" Another time he caught me in the corridor—"Did you know she is divided into sixteen watertight compartments, so that if she strikes anything, she can be sealed in minutes from the bridge?"

I began to get a little tired of it all. If he was so excited by the ship, perhaps I should offer the prize to him. But somehow, his excitement and that of the others in the home were starting to interest me. Perhaps there was something in the liner after all.

Each time that Raymond saw me, he handed me a piece of a paper with some new fact or other concerning *Titanic*. Then, one evening he gave me a pamphlet that he said I could keep and asked me at the same time, "Did you know that her centre anchor weighs more than fifteen and a half tons and it took a team of twenty horses to tow it to the shipbuilders?" He had a habit of asking the question but never waiting for the reply; in fact I was getting throughly sick of the sound of her name and starting to think seriously about returning the tickets to Southampton. Anyway, I decided to browse through the pamphlet and perhaps even find a fact that even Raymond was unaware of.

So as we all settled down in the dormitory, we were allowed to read for about half an hour before the lights were turned off. I started to read the pamphlet that Raymond had given me, having left my book downstairs. As I started to read, I could not help a twinge of excitement when I was reading some of her details and also about some of the most famous people of the day who would be her first passengers. Many were millionaires or important celebrities. When the lights in the dormitory were turned off, I found I wanted to read on, so I took my small torch under the bedclothes to read until all was silent and everyone else had gone to sleep. Eventually, I finished the booklet and turned off the torch to go to sleep.

Then I had the most amazing dream.

I dreamt of a great liner cruising majestically through calm and silent waters of a dark ocean. Music and laughter filled the air as the hundreds of passengers enjoyed themselves in the magnificent staterooms on board. The sea was beautiful and so calm, with hardly a wave breaking the surface. It was in fact like a polished mirror with the brilliant stars in the dark sky reflected in the water. Despite this tranquil scene, I felt uneasy in my dream. There was something out there in that peaceful scene, something I could not see, but menacing and coming closer all the time, some object that when it struck the ship caused the laughter and happiness to turn to cries of panic and fear.

In my dream there were cries of anguish and panic; the music still playing lively tunes, but the ship was sinking slowly and the sea, which had appeared such a short time before calm and tranquil, now was filled with turbulence. People crying out for help. Some were desperately trying to keep above the water as the cold took hold until they gradually gave up and sank below the surface. High up above the ships, rockets burst, looking like some macabre firework display. I felt fear so strong that you could almost reach out to touch it. Whatever had been in the water, had struck hard at the ship and then disappeared into the silent night as if it had never been.

I woke from the dream shouting in terror. A cold sweat had broken out on my forehead and the matron was bending over me, calming me and telling me that it was only a nightmare and not real.

For a long while after the matron had gone, I lay awake in the room silent but for the gentle sound of the other boys breathing steadily in their sleep. I closed my eyes, but the fear crept in again. I stared at the ceiling, ultimately relieved that it was only a dream and not reality; it had been so real, so terrifying. Then I must have fallen asleep, for when I opened my eyes again, the sun was streaming through the curtains and the sound of the early morning bell was ringing in my ears. Another day was about to start.

With a shock I realised what day it was. It was Tuesday, April 9, the day when I was going down to Southampton to visit *Titanic*. After all the fuss, I felt strangely excited and ready for my day out.

Two
The Tour of *Titanic*

At breakfast everyone was talking about *Titanic*. One of the staff produced a newspaper that had a full-cover photograph of the new liner that tomorrow would be setting sail on her maiden voyage to America. I had the chance to glance through the paper. I noticed a photograph from the year before when she was first launched in Northern Ireland. She certainly did not look very grand then, with no funnels and looking like some sort of stranded whale, but still a look of future majesty and importance.

After breakfast, one of the staff took me to the station in the horse and trap. I was given strict instructions on how to behave on the train and while at Southampton. Usually I would not have been allowed to travel alone, but luckily for me, the member of the staff who had been allocated to come with me, had fallen ill with flu that morning, so I was to be allowed to go alone. I waved as the horse and trap that had brought me, set off back to the home, leaving me to show the ticket that had been part of the prize to the station master.

The train was in the station already. I had just time to find a seat and settle down when the whistle blew and the train, with a great deal of smoke and noise, started to move out of the station. I felt really excited about my newfound freedom and lit up the cigarette that I had found stubbed out in an ashtray in the home, left by some careless visitor I expect, and carefully hoarded for this moment. I breathed in the smoke deeply. It tasted really good and I felt really wicked with myself and my behaviour. I thought I was alone in the carriage when a voice in the corner suddenly interrupted my thoughts. "Hey, lad, mind you don't burn your fingers!" I was really surprised and looked down to see that the cigarette had burned down almost to my fingers. I realised I must have been daydreaming, a habit that I was often being told off about at school, and had my knuckles wrapped many a time with a hard wooden ruler by the teacher in charge. I thought I was in trouble again, but the large man in the corner was only laughing.

"Where are you off to, son?" he asked.

"I've been invited to look around *Titanic*," I replied. "I don't expect you have heard of her?"

"Well, actually I am the chief engineer, so I must have heard of her," he replied laughing.

After that we got on famously. I made a new friend and even promised to visit him deep in the bowels of the engine room if I was allowed. His name was Bill, and he was one of the most important men on the ship, as he told me. Without him, they would have to row *Titanic* to New York, which would surely not suit all those rich, fancy millionaires they were to carry.

When we pulled into Southampton, Bill said good-bye to me and disappeared into the crowds.

I felt suddenly alone, amongst all the milling crowds of people who all appeared to know exactly where they were going. I left the train and made my way out of the station. I handed in my ticket and was warned I must be back in the station by six, as that was the last train of the day. As I came through the ticket barrier, I noticed a tall young officer sporting the uniform of the White Star Line. He asked me if I was the boy whom he had been sent to meet, and I replied I was that boy. He did not appear very pleased at the prospect of showing me around. He told me in an affected and slightly annoyed tone that *Titanic* was sailing the next day, and he felt he had more important things to do than show me around. This made me feel really guilty and I was all for turning around and heading home, but he explained that he had his duty to do, so he and I had better make the best of it. So during the journey to the dock, we both sat in silence.

As we entered the dock gates, the atmosphere somehow changed, and so did the mood of my companion. He introduced himself and told me to call him Francis for the day, as I had kept calling him "Sir," which he told me sounded a little pompous, and that we might as well enjoy the time we were to be together and make the most of it.

As we came closer to the dock, I felt a feeling of anticipation and growing excitement. To add to this, the sun came out from the dark, gloomy April sky and lit up the dockyard, which was all hustle and bustle as the great liner was readied for sea. The light appeared to fall on that particular part of the dock. I felt a lump come into my throat, as I saw in front of us the gigantic liner that I had come to look around. She was the most magnificent sight that I could possibly have imagined. I had, of course, seen pictures of her, but to see her in reality was another matter altogether.

As we left the taxi and started to head for the gangplank, I began to get an idea of just how vast she was. I looked up, and it seemed as if she reached for the clouds. She was a full seventy feet above my head, with more than ten decks reaching to the four great yellow funnels, which it was said could have held two steam locomotives each at the same time, and each emitting just a wisp of smoke. I wondered if Bill had arrived on board and was giving instructions to his men.

As I stared, dumbfounded at this magnificent sight, my

mouth wide open in astonishment, Francis, standing beside me, started to laugh.

"She is big, isn't she?" he said, " . . . and beautiful, a real queen of the ocean."

The Blue Peter flew at her yardarm, and on the masthead flew the house flag of the White Star Line, and then on the foremast the Stars and Stripes, showing her destination on the morrow was to be the New World. On her bows far above my head written in gold lettering was the word *Titanic*.

Francis took my arm and said, "Come on, dreamer. She is even more beautiful inside." I found this difficult to believe, but I would soon be pleasantly surprised. We made our way through the first-class entrance and down the grand staircase into the vast open hall-like area, which Americans call the lobby. We stopped to look around. Francis smiled at the look of amazement on my face. He, also, was enjoying himself, and in the short time he had been with the liner, he was becoming an avid fan. His mood had thawed and he was obviously enjoying himself. What he was telling me about the ship was spoken with pride and unknowingly instilling in me also a feeling of affection for this ship, a feeling that was to steadily grow as the day progressed.

Hanging above the grand staircase was a magnificent clock, which comprised two bronze figures symbolising "Honour and Glory Crowning Time." It was one of the finest clocks I had ever seen, and I made up my mind to make time to sketch it before the end of the day.

With Francis by my side smiling and obviously excited, he was determined to attempt to surprise me if he could, and with this intention, he could not fail, for in every room and at every turn, there was another surprise.

We set off along A-Deck and looked in the Reading and

Writing Room. Francis gave me a piece of the ship's writing paper to keep as a souvenir. It was embossed in gold lettering, with the name of the ship and the crest of the White Star Line. We looked at the lounge and the Palm Court and also in the first-class smoking room, all part of the privileges of the first-class passengers, who in a few hours time would be filling these silent rooms with their talk and laughter. Every turn and corner held an interest and fascination. It was amazing how big the ship really was. She was a floating city.

I asked Francis her measurements and he told me that she stood ten decks or eleven stories high. If stood on her end, as illustrated in several newspapers that I had seen recently, she would be taller than the new Woolworth Building in New York. Her four funnels, three for discharging steam and smoke and a dummy for ventilation, were each twenty-two feet in diameter and rose sixty-two feet above their casing. Her boilers provided the power (over 50,000 horsepower) to move the vessel at more than twenty-three knots or twenty-six miles an hour over the sea. She was the largest and one of the fastest passenger ships in the world. They also provided power for evaporation and refrigeration plants as well as for four passenger elevators, a fifty-telephone switchboard for ship use, and a five-kilowatt wireless telegraph station.

Deep under the water, in the very bowels of the ship were those twenty-nine boilers and one hundred and fifty-nine furnaces for providing the power for the ship and for the three large screws to drive her through the water.

Her hull was divided into sixteen watertight compartments. These were divided by fifteen transverse bulkheads. Her steel bottom was double skinned and reinforced with tons of concrete, making her, like her sister *Olympic,* a very safe ship, even considered by many "unsinkable"; it was thought that the sixteen conventional lifeboats and the four collapsible lifeboats would be sufficient for the two thousand or so on board, as they covered the Board of Trade recommendations and it was believed that they would never be needed, as nothing could damage this ship, except perhaps a torpedo, and Britain was not at war.

The rudder weighed one hundred tons and the three anchors, which were to bring her to rest, weighed more than thirty tons each. I began to realise more and more what a colossal ship this really was. I could quite believe Francis also, when he told me he was only just beginning to get used to the ship after the few days he had been on board for sea trials, as there were literally miles of passages and companionways, and it was quite possible to get lost on the ship.

For the passengers a large crew was needed, nearly four hundred in all, from officers to the engine-room crew for the ship, and for the hotel side, more than five hundred and eighteen who were responsible in their different capacities for the comfort and happiness of the two thousand four hundred or so passengers on board. In the bowels of the ship, the firemen were ready to stoke more than six hundred and fifty tons of coal into the furnaces each day to keep her sailing over the sea.

Francis and I continued our tour visiting the great staterooms, which were soon to be occupied by the greatest and richest people of the day. These were silent now, but being made ready for the expectant passengers with fresh flowers on the tables, chilling champagne, and the fireplaces filled with coal ready to be lit when the passengers were to board. These grand staterooms took up most of A as well as the B and C decks. At the end of B Deck was the magnificent First Class dining room, where even now the crew were preparing the tables, covering the wooden surfaces with snow-white tablecloths, and the glistening, polished, silver cutlery embossed with the White Star Livery emblem and the name of the ship. The dining-room staff, preparing for the first meal on board, looked to me like so many pagan priests and priestesses, all ready to take part in some sort of strange ceremony, in this quiet but magnificent room.

The crystal chandeliers, which would not look out of place in Buckingham Palace, glistened and glowed in the light as if alive. The air filled already with the fresh smell of flowers, all awaiting the imminent passengers to enjoy their first dinner with the resident orchestra playing classical or lively tunes to entertain them.

On the tour, Francis talked incessantly to me and introduced me to the different crew members whom we came across. We met so many that they began to become just a blur of faces and names. It was the ship herself that fascinated me and kept my interest sharp. I was becoming attached to her in a strange mysterious way. There was something in her magnificence and splendour that captivated my imagination. The next stop was the Millionaires Suites on B Deck; these were to be occupied at a cost of £850 for a single crossing, which was so vast a sum of money that I could not even imagine it. These rooms were completely self-contained. They even had their own strip of deck where one could sit out and walk without meeting any of the other passengers. The cabins themselves were magnificent, with double or single beds. I had always thought of a bedroom, or in this case cabins, as places just to sleep, but here they were works of art. Instead of the usual shipboard portholes, these rooms had windows that looked out over the ocean. Instead of ugly iron radiators for warmth, there were open grates, whose fires of bright blue and green from the sea coal would soon be blazing, as the rich passengers made themselves comfortable for the crossing of the Atlantic in a few hours' time. Each of the suites we visited was decorated in a different style and colour, each one completely unique.

On the Boat Deck high up on the ship, Francis showed me the Officers Quarters and a miniature golf course, where we had a game before continuing our tour. While we played, Francis mentioned that the richer people had their own servants and valets who had their own small cabins alongside the main suites. There was room also on the ship for cars to be brought and even a kennel on board.

As we made our way down the Grand Staircase again, Francis led me into what appeared to me to be a small room, about the size of the average box room. I could not for the life of me understand why he had brought me here and what the room was for, when all of a sudden, the room moved. I was terrified. Francis was watching me with pleasure. This was one of the new lifts. The *Titanic* had several, which made the transfer between decks so much easier. All the new buildings in New York had them, he said. After a while I overcame my fear, even though I felt we could fall to our deaths if something went wrong, as he told me that it was supported by only a thin wire and system of pulleys; but after going up and down a few times, I began to enjoy myself to no end, until an indignant bell boy asked us to move away.

After this experience, I found it difficult to imagine anything on the ship that was going to be as exciting, but I was wrong. Every turn and every new room I was shown held some new fascination. The First Class Dining Room, which was now ready for guests, took the breath away with its opulence. The vast kitchens, with food to cook for a whole city afloat, the fridges for the food and wine, and even a special cold room containing flowers, to ensure fresh flowers all the way to New York. A vast unsinkable city, which the builders had guaranteed could withstand whatever man or nature could throw at her.

I, like Francis, was starting to feel a deep affection for

the ship, a feeling difficult to put into words, but a feeling of pride and that somehow I belonged in some way to the future of this great "Queen of the Seas." And I knew from that moment that somehow I would do my best to stay with her and see the New World for myself. But I would have to formulate a plan, a plan that would work. Where could I stay hidden until we were well out into the Atlantic and not likely to be sent home? That meant staying hidden until we had left Southampton, then Cherbourg, and finally Ireland, before she would sail away from land towards New York.

While I secretly began to think up a plan, Francis showed me the gymnasium. Here he took off is jacket and demonstrated how the richer, more overweight passengers could lose weight by riding the mechanical camel or the horse. I rode one also. They were like the seaside mechanical ones that I had once ridden when visiting the seaside with my parents, but these were faster and much more fun, being designed for adults and not for children. For about half an hour, with no one else about, we both went quite mad, shouting and laughing with pleasure. I felt sure if the captain had come in at this time, he would find himself looking for a new officer.

After getting very hot, we returned for some fresh air to the Boat Deck, I raced Francis, but he managed to beat me and was not short of breath, so I suspected he had found a quicker route to the deck!

The life boats were looking so clean and white in their davits, but they made me feel a little uncomfortable. I thought back to the dream of the night before. There did not seem enough for all the passengers and crew on board. There was apparently no life boat drill for the crew, which seemed strange, but Francis told me there were enough life boats to cover the Board of Trade Regulations, even though I saw they could have fitted twice the number of davits with more boats. However, this would have restricted the space on this deck, and anyway, he pointed out that they would hardly be needed, as there was little chance of *Titanic* sinking.

I asked if the passengers were given any drill, but he smiled and told me the passengers had come on board to enjoy themselves on their voyage to America and did not want to be frightened by having a boat drill, which was sure to upset many of the more influential passengers, and would not help the advertisements, which stated that this ship was the best available for the North Atlantic in terms of luxury, service, and, of priority, safety.

I had heard stories about the North Atlantic being rough in a storm, and *Titanic* was crossing in the early spring, where patches of poor weather would be inevitable. Francis told me that she had stabilisers and, being such a large ship, she would not roll as smaller ships in heavy seas. Anyway the forecast for the crossing was good, and there was no poor weather predicted.

Francis showed me one of the life boats. He removed the protective tarpaulin cover so I could see the wooden seats and the oars tied up securely. Each boat had provisions and would be stocked with blankets at a moments' notice; he even showed me how the davits worked, and swung the boat over the side, but it was difficult as the paint on the davits had dried, making it a real struggle to get the machinery working. He eventually, with my help, managed this task, which showed they could be worked by one man. I looked out over the side and saw the seventy-foot drop below; it gave me quite a fright, my not having a very good head for heights. I was quite small, and ever since childhood, even stairs with gaps between had terrified me. I drew back quickly, and Francis grabbed hold of me and went as if to throw me over the side. He was laughing and I shouted in terror.

Francis was rambling on about the ship. I was only half-listening, still trying to work out a plan, for it was only a short time before I was due to leave to catch the train home. I had not seen the engine room yet, or Bill, and I would also have liked to see the bridge from which *Titanic* was controlled and where I could meet the fabled Captain Smith, who was the most famous captain of the White Star Line. He had been the captain of the *Titanic's* sister ship *Olympic*, and he had been asked to take charge for *Titanic's* maiden voyage. He was due to retire after this trip.

Francis took me for a slap-up meal in one of the dining rooms. The staff treated us like royalty. We were to be the guinea pigs before the main passengers came on board. After lunch, as promised, we made our way deep inside the ship to the boiler and engine rooms, where I met Bill again. He was really pleased to see me, and took me on a tour of his kingdom, which was a little different from the grandeur that I had already experienced.

His face was black and his hands oil-stained as he showed me round this vast area, which housed the great boilers. Men were already sweating, starting to fill the vast furnaces with coal from the mountains around them. It took several hours, apparently to build up the heat for the steam needed to drive the engines and the massive screws through the water in just a few hours time. We were due to sail at noon, so everything had to be ready for that time.

Bill gave me the tour, and soon I felt sweaty and very hot. He told me that *Titanic* had three main screws or propellers, which were to drive her through the water at twenty-three knots. The centre screw weighed twenty-two tons while the two wing screws weighed thirty-eight tons. They were made of bronze, which did not rust like other metals. The firemen I watched working so hard had to shovel more than six hundred and fifty tons a day into the furnaces to keep her running at top speed. What a contrast it was with the ship's elegance, this picture of hell, the furnaces blowing heat out and sending the light from the flames to climb the walls, reflecting bizarre and strange patterns on the bulkheads.

Just above the engine room was the Third Class dining room, protected from the heat and the noise by sheets of thick steel. Bill made a joke that he had better not get the furnaces too hot or they might burn the passengers' feet!

After saying good-bye to Bill, we headed up through the ship to the bridge, the control room of *Titanic,* where already there were officers on station, ready for the sailing time in just a few hours. The various charts and maps were laid out and the different flags and pennants ready to hoist on the morrow, as the mast heads would be a mass of colour when the passengers arrived. I did not meet Captain Smith, which was rather a disappointment, but I expected that pleasure would come before too long, especially if they discovered there was a stowaway on board. I had heard that he was a strict man, and some were afraid of him, but I felt no fear. Taking my punishment would be small fare compared to sailing the greatest ship ever built on her maiden voyage.

Not long after this tour, Francis took my arm and said it was time to leave the ship. He had enjoyed my company, and we both had a splendid day, but he had work to do and I had a long train journey home, so it was time to go. He did not have the time to see me to the station, but I assured him that I could easily find my way. For this I was relieved, as I did not want him coming and seeing me onto the train, or all my plans would be useless. He gave me some pamphlets and photographs of the ship before saying good-bye on the gangplank. He watched me go down to the dock, then he disappeared from sight.

I knew *Titanic's* first port of call was Cherbourg in France, and then to Ireland before setting out for New York. I would have to stay low until then, and I had by now made up my mind about a hiding place where I hoped no one would look for me if I was missed before *Titanic* was well out to sea. My hiding place was going to be a lifeboat, so I just hoped the weather would keep mild and not get too cold, or I would have to give up and was sure to be sent home.

It was just starting to get dark when I had left the ship, during that strange time of the day we call "twilight." I hid behind some crates and watched for my opportunity. The ship was now ablaze with lights as preparations continued for the next day's departure. There had been up to now always a seaman on the gangplank, checking all those who came on board, but now as I watched, he moved away, probably for a cigarette, and now I knew I had my chance. It was now or never. I felt afraid and my heart beat like mad.

I came out of hiding and ran as quickly as I could for the gangway, expecting the shout of discovery at any moment, but no one called and I was soon on the silent Boat Deck. Once I had to hide quickly in a doorway when I saw two stewards passing, but they were deep in conversation and did not notice me.

I reached the lifeboats and looked around. All was quiet as I quickly slipped under the tarpaulin cover. I lay still, my heart racing as I waited for someone to lift the cover and tell me to get out, but no one came and I started to relax a little. I found a blanket in one of the lockers, and I had a pack of sandwiches that Francis had given me when I left, so I should be all right for a while. I lay down on the bottom of the boat and in a few minutes was fast asleep after all the excitement of the long day and the expectation of the future and what lay ahead.

Soon dreams took over, and the boy lay still, unnoticed under the cover of the lifeboat. The golden lettering of the Titanic *on her prow appeared to glow as if alive under the light of the rising moon.*

Three
The Stowaway

I remember that first night so clearly, curled up in the lifeboat. I had been so tired after the long and eventful day. I had fallen asleep immediately. My dreams had come fast, strange confusing dreams, the events of the day all mixed up with pictures of my parents smiling and laughing on that last family holiday together before the accident in which they died.

The dream of the night before returned. The magnificent staterooms on *Titanic* filled with the wealthy, their valets and maids, scurrying back and forth, seeing to their masters' and mistresses' every whim. In the First Class dining room, the men were in evening dress, dark coats, and black bow ties. The ladies were in magnificent gowns, their jewellery reflecting the light from the crystal chandeliers, like a million brilliant stars, moving gently and majestically back and forth to the sound of a Strauss waltz.

The faces of the young couples were clean and healthy as they swirled in and out amongst the guests. Everyone appeared gay and happy. The world at that moment was perfect. England ruled the waves of the oceans and what could possibly go wrong? It was a world full of rich and wealthy people with few cares in the word. Here in the First Class of *Titanic,* the people were unafraid. The world in 1912 for the rich and privileged classes could not have been better.

All of a sudden in my dream, a dark cloud seemed to pass over this tranquil and safe scene; there was a slight shudder. One or two couples appeared to stumble and some looked a little shocked, but the music still played and no one really noticed. In my dream, now a dark shadow had come across the scene and everything had somehow changed. Something had happened that was to convert those cheerful, happy faces to panic, sadness, and great fear. In my dream, I could move unseen through the ship, passing from one deck to another without effort.

Below the First Class, deep in the bowels of *Titanic* were different people, families with strange sounding accents, and their clothes, in contrast to the magnificence of the First Class passengers, were threadbare and simple. These people were also dancing, not to a grand orchestra, but to a single man who was playing the fiddle. He was playing his instrument fast and everyone in the rooms was either dancing, singing, or tapping their feet to the beat. Even the thin, half-starved faces of the children looked cheerful and happy.

These were not the rich, pampered passengers. These had the weather-beaten faces of people who had suffered many hardships and disappointments, and many of the children were very thin and without shoes or socks.

Bottles were clinking together, and the air was filled with swirling tobacco smoke. These people, despite their worried faces, were enjoying themselves, singing and dancing as if they had no cares in the world, their moving shadows making strange shapes on the bulkheads in the reflected light from the lamps.

Some dark shadows passed again over my dream. I had a strong feeling of foreboding, as if a cloud had passed in front of the sun. All of a sudden, what I had feared was there. Seawater was pouring through gaps in the ship's side;

men, women, and children were calling desperately for help, many screaming in panic, as the ice-cold waters rose to drown their pitiful cries in an awful gurgling, spluttering sound, as the unmerciful water filled their lungs. The white angry water raged around them as they struggled in vain to get out, while the water, like some live hungry monster, swept away their bodies and their cares.

In my dream, I moved swiftly to the Boat Deck. The lifeboats were being swung out on their davits and being slowly lowered the seventy feet to the surface of the sea. Screams and cries for aid filled the dark night, all mixed with the prayers of those who asked for God's mercy on this terrible scene. Bright distress rockets reached high into the air. A high-pitched scream came from the funnels as the excess steam was released to prevent the boilers exploding when the cold sea water hit them.

I felt at that moment a great sadness and loneliness. My chest was tight with a terrible pain. I wanted to help these people so very much, but in my dream, I was powerless, just an observer of the terrible scenes being enacted out before my tear-filled eyes.

It was at that moment when I woke from my sleep, cold and shivering, sweat pouring down my face as the nightmare I had just lived seemed so real. For a moment I could not place where I was. Perhaps I was dead, drowned, and lying on the ocean floor. Then I saw the light from the early morning sun coming through the canvass tarpaulin. I almost cried out with relief to be in the lifeboat. I had not had such a real and terrifying dream since I was a small child.

All of a sudden, I felt a slight shudder which told me that *Titanic* was nearly ready to sail. I looked out carefully from the cover, taking care not to be seen, and watched the scene on the dock far below. Crowds of people were milling about, carriages were arriving and soon the boat train would be arriving with the passengers to start boarding. Mountains of luggage were being loaded into the side of the ship where massive doors had been opened to take in the luggage and the vast quantities of food and supplies that would be needed for the Atlantic crossing. Despite all the activity, there was a powerful feeling of expectation and excitement. This was the maiden voyage of the famous *Titanic*, largest and most luxurious ocean liner ever built, with a passenger list of rich and famous people who would not look out of place at a Buckingham Palace garden party. An orchestra and a band were already playing jolly ragtime music on the quay, as people started to board, waving to their friends and relations who were there to see them off on their voyage, not one aware that this was to be a voyage to eternity for most of those who came on board.

With all the activity and excitement, I wanted to jump from my hiding place and join in with all the fun, but I knew if I did that, I would soon be caught and put back on the train home, so I had to stay concealed until we were well away from land and that would not be for some time. I felt excited to be on board the largest and the proudest liner ever built, and about to make one of the most important voyages of her life, her maiden voyage to New York.

A few minutes before midday, I saw the crowds shouting and waving flags and bunting. The orchestra was playing sentimental tunes. I could see and hear the passengers all around me now calling and shouting their good-byes back down to the dock. The side of the ship was ablaze with streamers and coloured paper. Then I heard a voice shouting, which sent a shiver of excitement down my spine, "She's starting to move!" and there was a great shudder as the massive screw far below started to move slowly. The heavy hawsers were thrown into the sea, and the gap between the ship and the quay began to widen. I peered out of my small crack and tears filled my eyes with the sheer excitement of this moment, a moment in history.

We started to move slowly away from the dock, amidst all the excitement from both the ship and the quayside crowds. We moved slowly into the channel.

All of a sudden, there was a lot of shouting, and for a while, the ship appeared to slow down. It was not until much later that I found out what had happened, as the great liner had almost come to grief before even leaving port. Apparently, as *Titanic* had moved away from the dock, she had caused such a massive pull in the water that two other passenger ships moored across the water were straining at their moorings and could have collided with her. Before too long, however, the grand ship started to move again. We headed out into the Channel and towards the open sea.

Four
Cherbourg and Ireland

When we were safely away from the quay, and the engines had settled down to a steady rhythm, I looked out over the side. I could see people moving along the coast stopping to point and wave at us as we sailed majestically past. From the shore there could be no mistaking the four funnels of the most famous passenger ship afloat. The newspapers had been full of her pictures in the past few days.

It felt quiet, in contrast from all the excitement and noise when we departed a short time before. I imagined Bill, now tending his beloved engines. What a surprise he would have if he knew I was thinking of him just a few decks above. Perhaps I might surprise him with a visit later in the voyage. He was a great bloke and I was sure would not tell on me.

Just then I heard voices close by where I was hiding. I crouched down and held my breath. I was pretty safe here and secure. With no life boat drill, I was hardly likely to be disturbed, and if I was not yet reported missing, there would be little chance of anyone removing the cover. The voice that I had heard was of a man and woman talking and there was some concern in his voice. I decided to listen carefully to their conversation. They were discussing the near collision a few hours before.

"This was a bad omen, you know?" the man said. "Do

you love your life?" To which question, the lady replied that she did.

"Then take my advice and leave *Titanic* at the first opportunity; I certainly shall. I am going to disembark at Cherbourg and wait for another ship to New York."

The lady laughed, but not in any sarcastic way. She mentioned that they were both on one of the fastest and safest ships afloat and asked why was he afraid, but I did not hear any more of the conversation as they moved farther up the deck.

As they passed out of earshot, I felt a strange shiver down my spine and the expression "An angel has passed overhead" came to my mind. For a while, my cheerful mood changed to one of thoughtfulness, but I did not fear bad omens and dismissed the man's conversation as just superstition. I had come to feel a great admiration for this ship and was feeling both very excited and guilty to be here on board and not back at home, where by now they must be starting to get more than a little worried about me. The ship also had the new radio, so I was a little afraid as to how long it would be before the ship was called and a search would start to look for me.

The fear of that moment quickly passed away. I once more looked out on that bright sunny April afternoon and felt a slight shudder as *Titanic* picked up more speed and headed out of the Channel towards the coast of France and our first port of call, Cherbourg.

It was only recently that the new passenger liners had started to use Southampton as their base, moving to France to pick up the lucrative American tourists and businessmen.

In the First Class dining room, lunch was being served. I could hear the sound of the orchestra playing as the passengers dined, and for the first time on board, I felt hungry, but I knew it would be a while before I dare show my face. I still had the sandwiches and some lemonade, which Francis had given me yesterday, so I tucked in with an appetite. Perhaps it would be safer after dark when there were fewer people around and I would not be so easily recognised.

I lay still in the shelter of the life boat. The sunshine filtered through, making my home cozy and quite warm, but I could not help but worry a little about the weather, as it could be very rough and cold out in the open Atlantic. At least for now, here in my hiding place I was quite sheltered. I opened up some of the cupboards under the seats and found a few blankets that would help to make me more comfortable. Soon with the distant sound of the orchestra and the gentle beat of the engines far below me, I drifted to sleep.

Some time later I woke, and heard the rustle of tea cups. It must have been about four o'clock and tea time. Had I really been asleep for all those hours? I felt refreshed and peered out of the cover to see the coast of France coming closer, with a few distant houses.

Before long *Titanic* began to slow down. The engines took on a more gentle beat. We eventually stopped and a hasty movement of passengers and luggage took place. I could not help but wonder if the gentleman whom I had overheard earlier was disembarking and if the lady he was in conversation with had taken his advice and left the ship also. I supposed I would never know. The air was fresh and the seagulls wheeled overhead, amazed at this giant manmade monster, which reached so high into the sky. They called more as the cook threw overboard some of the vast quantities of garbage that such a great city generated.

After a short while, the throb of the engines told me that we were underway once more. This time there was only one more call to make, and that was in Queenstown in Ireland. Then, we would set sail for New York and the New World.

After Ireland, I could look for somewhere better to stay, somewhere that would be warmer before we set out into the cold North Atlantic. Francis had told me that Captain Smith was going for the 'Blue Riband,' which was to see if we could cross the Atlantic in the fastest time. I hoped we would have a chance. And why not? We were one of the fastest liners afloat. I determined now to keep low, and, if I did look out, to make sure it was on the seaward side with less chance of being spotted. I certainly did not want to be discovered now, and I certainly wanted to accompany *Titanic* on her maiden voyage.

Titanic had now taken on her full complement of First and Second Class passengers, although a few might join the Steerage passengers who were due to board at Queenstown. She held now some of the most famous and wealthiest people in the world.

It was that night when I met Howard for the first time. He would be the first person I would talk to since boarding the liner. It happened before we reached Queenstown in Ireland. I was by this time very hungry, so I decided to sneak out to try to find the kitchens to get something to eat. Francis had taken me there, but his directions were rather hazy, as when I had visited, I did not fully expect at that time to still be on board. Anyway I would have to take extreme care, because if Francis or any other of the other crew I had been introduced to were to see me, it would be curtains and I would be taken off at Queenstown. I also remembered that the Officers Quarters were on the Boat Deck, so again I would have to be extremely cautious.

At about two in the morning, I awoke feeling cold and hungry. *Titanic* was quiet now, although never completely silent. There were always those passengers who did not go to bed, they liked to sleep in the daytime—the "night owls" of the ship, who played cards, danced, or talked through the night. I knew I was better off to stay where I was, but with the smell of the food coming from the First Class Dining Room all evening, I was by now pretty ravenous, hungry enough to take a few risks. What I was hoping for, was that if I was seen, I could be taken as any of the other children on board, although my clothes were rather old-fashioned and a little threadbare.

Quickly and quietly I made my way to the companionway. I eventually located the dining room area, quiet now, with the crystal chandeliers glinting in the pale light, reflecting the shiny silver of the knives and forks laid out for breakfast in the morning. Although it was semidark, I still felt as if a million eyes were out there watching me. I expected at any moment to hear a voice shatter the stillness and declare that I had been found out. Somehow, miraculously to me, I remained undetected and managed to discover the great swinging doors that led into the kitchen.

The kitchen was still and quiet. I knew it would not remain so for very long, as long before dawn the bakers would be preparing the bread and cakes for the day's breakfast; the kitchens were rarely deserted. Plates were piled high, beautiful pure white china with the magnificent insignia of the White Star Line and *Titanic* emblazoned on each. I saw a tray of leftover bread rolls, with a saucer of butter, each piece curled into a fantastic shape by the butter curlers. I munched happily away, hoping no one would notice the rolls that were missing. I also found a trifle in one of the fridges, a wonderful work of art in its own silver bowl. I stuffed it down, and carefully cleaned out the bowl. I washed the food down with some milk that I found, drinking straight from the jug, so as to leave no telltale traces. I now stuffed my pockets with bread and biscuits and started to make my way back to the dining room. It was at this moment when I felt a strange sensation. I knew I was being watched, and in horror, I realised that I was not alone. I turned around sharply, and there standing not more than ten feet away was another boy, dressed in pyjamas and a bright red ressing gown; it must have been the bright red colour that attracted my eye. I looked and wondered if it was worthwhile dashing for the door to escape, I would look rather suspicious if I ran, so I decided too brazen it out, and anyway, what was he doing there at that hour? I stared at him hard and slowly, ever so slowly. His tongue came out and wagged at me in a cheeky manner. I could have clocked him one on the jaw, but instead I laughed out loud, so much so that I was sure someone would hear us and we would be discovered.

Soon we were talking and laughing like old friends. After a while I began to wonder how I was going to get rid of him, or at least give him the slip, in case he followed me back to the lifeboats. Eventually, my chance came when he disappeared into the kitchen, looking for an ice cream. I slipped out and made a dash for the Boat Deck. I found it easy, as now I knew where I was heading, so in minutes and after a quick look around, I slipped back under the cover and curled up in the blankets, feeling warm and much better after my feed. I was soon asleep, gently calmed by the steady drone of the engines far beneath my hiding place.

I did not sleep very well. The dreams came again. This time I saw my new friend Howard struggling in the water. It was freezing as I could see ice floating on the surface, and he had a coating of frost on his eyebrows. He was calling for help. Everywhere were pieces of debris and flotsam. Howard cried in fear, but as in my last dream I could not help. All I could do was watch. I awoke, sweating freely and trembling with fear.

Later, when I slept again, another dream disturbed my

rest. This time I was in a boat in the water; it was the same lifeboat that I was now hiding in. All around in the freezing water, were people crying out for aid. The sound of spluttering and choking as many drowned. The terrible thing was that, again, I was powerless to help. It was as if I were paralysed and could only watch in horror as many disappeared beneath the cold, smooth surface.

After this dream had wakened me, I decided to try to stay awake for a while. It was that quiet, cold time just before dawn breaks. The light was just appearing on the far horizon. As I watched the dawn begin to break, I noticed the red streaks reach across the sea, as the early morning sun began to rise above the horizon. Today was going to be a day of decision. I would do my best to remain undetected until we had left Ireland. Then I should be safe. I wondered if there had been any messages about me telegraphed to the ship, and if there would be police waiting at Queenstown to search the ship looking for me, for I must have been missed by now. If all proved okay, I would need to find somewhere warmer and safer for the days we would be in the open Atlantic.

Just before forenoon, I heard the voice of the lookout far above my head in the forward crow's nest, and looking out over the seaward side I saw in the distance, the grey, windswept mountains of Cork, at the southern tip of Ireland. The mountains looked as if they had just been created, a green emerald island, beautiful with the suns rays slanting over the peaks, emphasising the different shades of green, all contrasting with the blue and green of the sea.

For the first time in many hours, the engine began to slow, as *Titanic* approached the Duant light vessel, moored a few miles south of Queenstown, where we were to take on the pilot. After slowing to pick him up, we carried on slowly towards port. I wondered if at that moment there was a shipboard search going on, looking for me. If that was so, I was determined to make the most of every moment I was on board *Titanic*.

The sounding lines were being dropped as we came nearer to the land, and I could hear the seamen calling out the fathoms. We steamed slowly through the Heads, rounding the low lying Roche's Point, with its lighthouse and signal towers. And then finally we anchored two miles from shore. We were too large a vessel to dock or get any closer to land without damage in the shallow waters.

Before long, two tenders, the *Ireland* and the *America*, came alongside bringing huge bags, of what presumably were mail bags, bound for America. With the mail came some more passengers. These were in contrast to the passengers whom I had seen before, with their mountains of luggage and their servants. These were for the most part young people leaving Ireland and their homes forever, in the hope of finding a new and better life as immigrants in America, the land of opportunity. Here in the New World anyone could become rich with the right talents and hard work, but others could easily die in poverty, seeking out a living in the vast slums of the larger cities, too poor to afford the passage back home.

For an hour, the "bumboats" came alongside the liner. These held local peddlers who were determined to make a sale to the rich clientele on board. Irish lace was the most popular of the goods on offer, and many were bargaining from the upper decks. When at last all the mail and the last passengers had boarded, the siren sounded, with all visitors being warned to go ashore. Then the giant anchors were raised and the engines began to throb. The steam whistles on the funnels let out an enormous screeching sound, as *Titanic* turned and headed out into the North Atlantic. No more ports of call until America, three thousand miles of open sea, and many days travelling before land would be sighted once again.

I saw the coast of Ireland become fainter, and I felt a great exhiliration as I realised I was free. I had not been discovered. They would surely not now turn around for one small unimportant orphan boy. I heard the bugle sound for dinner. It would soon be dark, and I would have to take my bearings and decide on somewhere else to stay for the remainder of the voyage.

Five
Out into the Atlantic

I began to feel a little out of place on this enormous ship and decided to go and find the one person whom I knew as a friend, and that was Bill, deep down in the bowels of the ship, somewhere far below, tending his beloved engines.

Titanic was a real maze, and it took me some time to find my way down through the ten decks and many long corridors to the engine room, well below the water line. The only lights down here were artificial and the light from the flames of the huge furnaces feeding the ever-hungry boilers. Every now and then, the door to a furnace would open to allow the stokers to shovel in more coal to the voracious flames. The strong, black-faced stokers sweated freely in the intense heat, as they shovelled in the coal, which was providing the power to carry *Titanic* through the waters of the North Atlantic at quite considerable speed.

After some time, I at last found a door, which led onto a kind of high platform, which looked down on the engine room below. The space large enough to hold the massive boilers was as vast as a cathedral. I looked carefully at the blackened faces, sweating below me, looking for the familiar figure of Bill. Then a hand rested on my shoulder and I thought I was done for. A well-known voice said, "Edward, is that you?"

I replied it was. He was surprised to see me and even

more surprised when I told him what I had done, to stow away, and I asked if he would now deliver me to the captain. He told me he would have to, but first we would have a chat over a cup of tea, before I would learn my fate.

Bill led me to the floor of the engine room, and we walked over a mountain of coal, a mountain that he informed me would become less as we made our way over the Atlantic. He told me also that they had a small problem, as it was suspected that some of the coal could have ignited nearer the bottom of the pile. Care would have to be taken to shift it to put out any fire due to combustion. He led me to a corner where there were a few packing cases arranged in a semicircle. He took an immense, blackened kettle and placed it near one of the furnaces. It was soon boiling and he made the tea in a large pot, as black with coal dust as the kettle. He offered me the tea in a battered china mug, and I drank gratefully. I tucked in greedily to the sandwiches he offered me along with a huge slice of fruit cake, which he told me that his wife had given him before he had left England.

Over the tea, I told him how I felt for *Titanic* and how I had stowed away in the lifeboats. He laughed and told me he would have done exactly the same thing thirty years ago if he had been in my position. He also said that with the weather becoming increasingly colder as she headed out into the open ocean, it was no good staying hidden in the lifeboats. Other, warmer accommodations would be needed. It was better to make a clean breast of what I had done and go to see Captain Smith, who was, Bill said, a good man. They were hardly likely to return back to port now, and he might even find me a job so I could work my passage, which was what I wanted very much. It was, Bill said, a grand life working on the great liners, and, if I worked hard,

I might even get a permanent job, which would be a good start towards a long and successful career.

I persuaded Bill to come with me to see the captain; and, with the first call to be the bridge, we made our way up through the giant ship, going from the very bottom to the very top. As we entered the First Class areas, passengers stood and stared at the ill-matched couple, the boy looking thin and forlorn, and the giant, black-faced engineer in oil-stained overalls.

On our entering the bridge, the captain called us into a small office. Bill had phoned ahead to say we were coming and the reason, so the captain was ready to receive us. We would also be away from the eyes of the other officers on the bridge. As we walked along, I saw Francis out of the corner of my eye. He looked quite startled to see me again. I had to remember to tell the captain that he had nothing to do with my coming back on board ship.

After entering the small office, we sat down and faced the captain.

"Well, Bill, how are you?" he said. "Are your wife and children well?" And as Bill and Captain Smith chatted without looking in my direction, I had time to look at this great man. I liked him straight away. The man before me he had gentle blue eyes that were full of humour. His skin was red and weatherbeaten—a real man of the sea.

Bill replied to the questions, "Very well, thank you, sir; congratulations for the command of *Titanic*. You must be very proud, and of course you were the best captain for the job!"

The captain smiled and then asked what he could do for Bill. With the sudden call from the engine room, he had been a little afraid there might be something wrong with the engines, at which Bill reassured the captain that the engines were running perfectly. He then proceeded to tell the captain of how he had met me on the train down to Southampton, and that I had come to him to make a clean breast of stowing away. The captain without any hesitations said, "Well, Edward, there is only one thing I can do for you. That is to have you walk the plank, but I shall have to wait until dark so as not to alarm the passengers. We could, on the other hand, keelhaul you. That would be fun. What do you have to say for yourself?"

I did not know what to say. I just felt terrified. Then I saw the corners of his eyes start to twinkle. He started to laugh along with Bill. He took out of a drawer a bottle of whisky, pouring a generous drop for Bill and even some for me, with plenty of water added. They sipped their drinks and I followed them. I had never tasted whisky before, and it burned my throat and started me coughing like mad. After a while we talked, and the captain decided to let me share a cabin in the crew's quarters and, as Bill predicted, the captain would let me know what duties I was expected to do to help pay for my keep and the passage on *Titanic*.

After an hour or so, I felt really tired. Bill showed me to the crew's quarters, and I straight away fell asleep on the bunk that I had been allocated. He said good-bye and disappeared back down to the engine room. He said that I could visit him at any time I liked.

When I woke, it was daybreak on the thirteenth of April. We were by now well out of sight of land and well out into the Atlantic. At least the captain had not turned around to take me back to England. I looked out over the stern at the white wake, with seagulls screaming, diving to pick up any waste that was being thrown overboard. The weather was fair, and the sea looked calm and still. I was amused to see some passengers jogging round the ship, some of the richest and most important people in the world, panting and looking very unfit. Others had wrapped themselves up and were sitting in deckchairs watching the ocean and the other passengers as they strolled past.

After a good lunch with the captain on the bridge, which gave us both a chance to talk to each other, he gave me a stern lecture on my behaviour and outlined a part of my duty, which was to assist the crew wherever I was needed. Francis would let me know what specific tasks I was to do. I spoke to him also. He was at first pretty annoyed with me, but he thawed and we got on well after that. He showed me the workings of the bridge and the heavy wooden wheel and the compass. He also showed me the course that we were taking from England to New York and the markings of various warnings of ice, which had been coming in during the night. These were all marked carefully on the charts so that a route could be planned that would be the safest for the passengers on board.

I was given permission to visit Bill in the engine room and so found my way back down. There was a sort of problem, which the captain wanted information on, a difficulty that was hard to talk over on the phone, so I went down to find out what it was and then to report back to the captain.

As Bill had told me before, they had discovered that a fire had broken out under the mountain of coal. Stokers were carefully removing what they could of the top layers, taking care not to let too much air in, which would ignite the fire even more. Fire on a ship was one of the most serious and feared nightmares, so I was shown what was taking place and then reported back to Captain Smith. He ordered the coal to be well watered down to damp the seat of the fire. He asked for reports every few hours.

I had time later in the day to have a bath and get rid of the coal dust, which was a major irritation to me. Then I met part of the crew, who on the whole, accepted me very well, even adopting me as a lucky mascot, which was all good fun. At least I now had somewhere to sleep and a meal inside of me twice a day. I was also on *Titanic*, which I was very pleased about indeed.

That night I spent some time with the lookouts, as icebergs could be in the area. Then I went to bed and slept really well. The next day was the fourteenth, and we had been warned of ice up ahead, so we would have to take care. As I looked out over the ocean, it looked peaceful and calm, with no sign yet of any bad weather or ice. I believed we were sailing at full speed. The bows were pushing white foam into mountains, and I saw at one point several dolphins keeping pace with the liner, which was really exciting.

Six
That Fateful Night

As the evening drew on, the day had seemed rather short. Those passengers who had braved the deck for a while retired back to their cabins or into the restaurant and dining rooms for dinner. Everyone appeared in high spirits and excited to be on board such a distinguished ship and on the way to the New World.

I had decided to join the look out that night and climbed the steep spiral staircase to scramble into the Crow's Nest without falling to the deck many feet below. Two of the crew had taken up stations and I knew them both. One was Fleet and the other Lee. They had asked me during the day if I would like to join them on the lookout, which I said I did. I had to keep my head down fairly well, for if Captain Smith spotted me, he could be quite angry. It was, however, getting gradually darker, and there was little chance of that.

The two men greeted me heartily and offered me some tea from a flask. They appeared a little uneasy, because they had been told to keep a sharp eye out for ice; but the sea was very calm and still, and we appeared to be moving very fast through the water.

They explained about icebergs, that they were often difficult to spot, as nine-tenths of the berg were usually below the water, and also to watch for "growlers," which were bergs almost completely submerged. Thus to spot them would be difficult, their presence evident only by a small fleck of white foam as the sea washed over them. The other problem, which Fleet pointed out to me, was that on a night like this, it was even more difficult to spot a berg. With such a clear night and the sea so calm, it was difficult to see where the ocean finished and the horizon started. They were glad that I was there with them, as extra eyes were all a help. Neither of the crewmen had any binoculars. They were part of the equipment that was not picked up before the liner set sail.

At about 10:30 P.M., Fleet spotted a ship going in the opposite direction. He told us it was the Furness Withy vessel, *Rappahannock*. As she came closer, she signalled to us. Fleet translated, "We have just passed through a heavy field of ice and several icebergs." We looked for a reply from the bridge and soon the light flashed back in Morse: "Message received. Thanks. Good night."

Lee said to us that soon we would feel *Titanic* slow down, especially with the fear of icebergs; we could even stop until daybreak to be on the safe side. As the minutes ticked by, we felt no change of rhythm in the engines far below. We wondered why. Perhaps Captain Smith had not yet received the message or the Chairman of the White Star Line, who was on board, Sir Bruce Ismay, had told him not to slow down, but that seemed unlikely, as on the high seas the captain was always the master.

As we watched in silence, straining our eyes to look over the silent, shadowy sea, I had a feeling of foreboding. I shivered as I remembered my dream, and the fear of something out there in the water, something very dangerous, which was drawing closer all the time. Lee saw me shiver and offered me a hot mug of tea. He assumed it was the cold that had affected me.

Gradually, as the time passed, I relaxed a little, but I still worked with the other two to keep our eyes searching all the time for something that might be amiss in the still night. Lee pointed out the thin mist that had formed over the surface of the water. This was starting to thicken, making it even more difficult to spot any "growlers" out there in the water. Fleet passed round the flask of hot tea, I could have gone to bed and left them to the watch, but nothing would tear me away until dawn broke and the daylight would make watching so much easier.

I started to think of my new friend, Howard, whom I had met earlier in the day. He had been very amused when I later told him about stowing away, and he took great pride in introducing me to his parents, stating he was the first person on board to know me before I was discovered. He appeared to me a lonely sort of figure. He had rich parents and everything he wanted, but he could not mix with other children and his stern governess gave him little time for himself away from his studies.

Time passed slowly, with all three of us straining hard with our eyes. It would not be safe to let up even for a moment. It was getting a lot colder now, and we wrapped ourselves up well in our thick coats and scarves. Lee told us it was a few minutes before eight bells. Soon we would be relieved and could go back to the warmth of our bunks. In a few hours, it would be daylight. Suddenly, Fleet's voice broke the silence; he spoke clearly and calmly. He had spotted something out there in the water. He reached for the phone link to the bridge, and the words I heard him utter sent a shiver of dread down my spine: "Iceberg dead ahead!" He put down the phone and took up his position. We all strained into the darkness, then the shock hit me like a sledgehammer. I saw it—a massive, gigantic, dark shape, barely visible straight in our path. To me then it looked extremely close. We were rushing towards it at great speed. I knew then that we could not avoid it.

Through the darkness, I distinctly heard the bells on the bridge ringing, calling for all engines to stop, and then calling for full astern. *Titanic* shuddered beneath our feet, and slowly, ever slowly, as if in slow motion the great liner began to turn to port. But straight ahead the berg was still there, more visible now and rushing towards us as if it were alive, some huge white monster determined to send us to our fate before we knew what was happening.

I knew we would strike, and we braced ourselves for the impact. We held on, knowing we could be thrown out of the Crow's Nest. Below I heard the alarms ringing, which were signalling that the watertight doors were being closed and the ship secured. For a few seconds, which seemed like hours, we stood still watching with horror and fascination as the berg drew closer; below the orchestra played on. No-one amongst the passengers appeared aware of the danger; laugher and conversation filled the night air, as the last passengers made their way to their cabins after the evening's entertainment.

Then the cold hit us, and I nearly fainted with the shock of it. Lee and Fleet were staring straight ahead with a look of sheer astonishment and fear on their faces. As *Titanic* moved more to port, I saw the massive berg slide past, and, for a few moments, I thought it had missed us. And then felt a slight shudder and heard the ominous grinding and scraping noise, like a giant tin opener far below us under the waterline.

I leaned out and saw the gigantic shape of the iceberg disappear into the darkness as if it had never existed. Then there was silence, a stunning silence, followed up by the sound of the alarm bells still ringing in my ears. The ship had stopped. It was still in the water. I felt amazed that no one appeared to have noticed what had just taken place, although most of the passengers would be in bed and the shudder of the iceberg passing was so slight that most would not have noticed it at all. I could hear the orchestra playing in the distance, and the sound of laughter still filled the air. I could also now see some passengers fooling around with the ice that had littered the forward part of the ship; they were getting together to play a game of football with it.

I left Fleet and Lee still standing and staring like statues at where the iceberg had disappeared to into the darkness. I nearly slipped in my rush to descend the narrow staircase to the deck below. For a moment I was unsure of what to do first. Then I knew I would wake Howard and tell him what had occurred. I felt I needed a friend at that moment. I was in a state of shock.

I made my way below, passing one or two sleepy-eyed passengers, who were standing in the corridors or talking to the stewards who were reassuring them and telling them to get back to bed. The strange thing that I noticed was the silence after the engines had stopped and the calm on the ship—no raised voices or panic, but I felt unsure. I knew something had taken place that was to change all our lives in a very short time.

Seven
Women and Children First

I roused Howard from a deep sleep. He came to the door of the cabin, looking sleepy-eyed, wondering whatever was the matter.

"Hello, Edward, how come you are not asleep?" he asked.

"I've been with Lee and Fleet in the Crow's Nest. We've struck an iceberg. Come on, we'll see if there is any damage."

Howard quickly got dressed and joined me. We made our way through the silent ship. It was strange not to hear and feel the reassuring steady beat of the engines below our feet. Passengers were standing in groups in their dressing gowns, others in evening dress, wondering just what was going on. The stewards were telling everyone everything was alright and to go back to bed.

I told Howard that we would go down to the engine room to see Bill. He would know what was happening, so we steadily made our way deeper and deeper into the ship. As we passed from passenger-only to crew-only areas, we saw no one to stop or challenge us. At times we had to lift the rope barriers dividing the different classes and the crew from the passenger accommodations, but I knew *Titanic* fairly well by now and found my way fairly easily.

We passed two stewards at one point. They were deep

in conversation and took no notice of us as we walked past them. Part of their conversation drifted to us.

"They say the water is rising fast; it is up to F Deck already, and the mail room is under water, with letters and parcels floating everywhere!"

Howard caught my eye. He gave me a frightened smile, and we continued without another word farther and farther, deep into the bowels of the stricken liner.

As we came closer to the engine room, we heard a terrific screaming noise as if a hundred steam engines were bearing down upon us.

"They must be releasing the steam from the boilers," Howard said. I had not realised the significance of this until I remembered the red-hot furnaces and boilers. If the ice-cold sea water entering *Titanic* touched them, there would be a great explosion, and surely rip a hole in the ship's side, which would mean we could sink in minutes.

As I opened the upper door to the engine room and looked down from the high platform to the room below, I saw sheer pandemonium—a scene from one of those Renaissance pictures that I had seen in books, of hell itself. The doors to the furnace were open and men were shovelling out their hot coal and ash; the heat was terrific. I could not imagine how they could stand the heat and the smoke down there on the deck. The fires were sending dark shadows and flaring multicolored lights all over the grimy bulkheads.

Bill saw us then and charged up to meet us, "What are you two doing here? Get back on deck as soon as you can. *Titanic* is doomed. We will try to keep her afloat for as long as we can, but I am not sure how long that will be. She is sinking hard by the head, and the pumps are not coping with the amount of water entering the ship. You best get up to the Boat Deck and get into a lifeboat as soon as you can!"

I asked Bill if he would come with us. He told us he

would come as soon as he could, but the boilers had to be cooled first, and he needed to keep the main generators working so the ship would have power for light and the radio. I suddenly realised that I would never see Bill again. He was not going to come up from the engine room as long as there was work to do there. I could not help but burst into tears and put my arms around his waist. He looked upset and pushed us out of the door back up the companionway to the upper decks. Before leaving he gave me a last hug and pushed a letter into my hand. He said it was a quickly written note for his wife and children, and that if I survived, I was to see she got it. I promised I would see to the letter and said with tear-filled eyes that we would see him soon on the Boat Deck; he was too young to die in the stomach of a great metal sea monster like this. He laughed.

As he turned, he saw how upset I was and said, "Remember, Edward, I promised you a model of *Titanic*, didn't I? Well, I never break a promise, so see you later. Now get going and don't hang about." She had not long to go now.

With that parting remark, he turned and made his way back to stand alongside his men, busy cooling down the massive fifteen-ton boilers.

So, taking Howard by the shoulder, I led him as we made our way back through the ship. Howard was crying quietly. We reached the cabin door of Howard's parents' cabin and it was some minutes before they could be persuaded to get up and take what we had told them seriously. It was not until a vase, which had been on the dressing table, all of a sudden began to slide and fell to the floor of the cabin with a crash, that they needed no further persuading. Donning their life jackets, they followed us as we all made our way up to the Boat Deck.

By now there were other people making their way to the top deck, most dressed in variety of different clothes, some fully clothed with furs wrapped around themselves, others in dressing gown and pyjamas. Many of the passengers appeared confused and even in some cases angry at being awakened and asked to go to the Boat Deck. Hardly anyone realised it was a real emergency. This was the unsinkable *Titanic*. Surely nothing could happen that would harm her. According to one lady passenger, the ship had no right to sink during the hours of darkness and while out of sight of land. We both smiled and wondered if she would be claiming her money back if the ship did not sink. Perhaps, we thought, *Titanic* might not be mortally injured and could stay afloat until rescue came and everyone could be taken off without having to get into the lifeboats. We were in fact only a day or two from New York. We could be towed easily. These hopes were soon dashed as we saw the lifeboats being swung out on their davits. I saw Francis and asked him just how serious the situation really was. He said it was very serious. *Titanic* had about two hours left before she would sink. The water gushing through the bow plates was proving too much for the pumps. She was doomed, and it was best if we found a place in one of the lifeboats as soon as possible. He reminded me of the fact that there were far too few lifeboats for those on board and many would be left to fend for themselves when the last boat left.

The scene on the Boat Deck looked rather confusing. The crew were attempting to swing out the boats from davits, which had been painted up. There had also not been any lifeboat drill, so neither crew nor passengers knew what to do in such an emergency as this.

At last the boats were starting to be lowered. They were lowered to a deck below the Boat Deck, which was considered easier for the passengers to board from. Despite this, it was still quite a terrifying experience to climb into an open boat, with a gap that showed the dark Atlantic seventy feet below. Some passengers refused to go when they saw what they had to do. Many still thought this was just a drill.

The women and the children were asked to get on board the lifeboats first. Then they were lowered to the sea surface below. As I waited with Howard and his parents, I looked around at the heartbreaking scene, as the deck had filled with people. Distress rockets soared into the clear sky, and at last the scream from the boilers stopped, causing for a few moments a unearthly silence.

There was one woman hugging her husband and refusing to leave him. They had been together all their lives and did not want to be parted now. I believed they were the Strauss couple, millionaire owners of the famous Macy's Store in New York. Other women were refusing point blank to leave the ship without their husbands, many choosing to stay together rather than be parted. I overheard a member of the crew trying hard to persuade a lady to enter a boat, but she would not go without her lucky charm, which was a china pig. In the end she retrieved it and went aboard a boat. Many believed that it was foolish to get into a boat, as all would soon be rescued. They could even see a ship's lights on the horizon less than ten miles away. There was certainly a feeling of hope amongst all this hopelessness.

As a distress rocket soared into the sky and burst into a multitude of colours, a sight that would have been wonderful in any other circumstances, the women and children were being taken off the ship, many in tears at leaving their husbands and fathers behind; the lines of lifeboats became shorter and shorter as they were being lowered and rowed away from the ship's side. People were crying. It was a heartrending scene, which will remain in my memory for the rest of my life. Suddenly another rocket soared overhead, with a terrific whoosh of sound, and then the band, led by Wallace Hartley, started to play lively ragtime tunes to keep up the morale of the people.

Then it came to our turn. There was an officer beckoning me to enter the boat with Howard and his mother. His father had just given a last kiss to his wife, when the officer looking around the deck where there were few waiting now, told him he could get in with his wife, as had some other men to take up more room as the boat was only about half full. I went to get in when Howard called me, but I felt a terrible feeling at that moment of desolation. These were not my family. I had no one, I should not be even on *Titanic,* and I felt did not deserve a place in the lifeboat. I turned and walked away, with Howard's voice calling in my ear as the lifeboat they were in was lowered to the surface. I felt tears of self-pity fill my eyes, but I wiped them away angrily with my sleeve. This was no time for self-pity. It was a time for courage.

I was just leaving the Boat Deck when I bumped into Francis. He started to tell me off for leaving the boats, but when I explained how I felt, he gave me a hug and said no more. There were many people who needed help and we would do what we could in the short time left. My first thought was for Bill. He would be, I knew, still at his station in the engine room, seeing that there was still sufficient power for the generators, so that the lights would still be working on the ship and that the radio room would still have power to keep sending their distress calls for help.

Eight
The Final Plunge

As we walked along the now silent, deserted companionways, I could feel the steady heel of *Titanic* as it settled even more by the bows. In places we came across passengers dressed in a variety of clothes, some wearing their life jackets, others holding them under their arms. We came to the broad thoroughfare known as 'Scotland Road' named after the famous street in Liverpool. Here were some of the strange looking and sounding people I had not seen since Queenstown, they were the steerage passengers. They were desperately looking for their way up to the Boat Deck, unaware that already there were few if any of the lifeboats left. They hardly gave us a glance and not a word passed between us as they continued to push their way aft.

Before too long we discovered that we could not go any further, the watertight doors and the rising water were barring our way. Bill must by now either have made it to the top of the ship or still down in the bowels of the ship where now he had little chance of being saved. Francis told me that by now *Titanic* had little time left to live, and so it was better for us both to return to the Boat Deck and to do what we could for those still left on board, which would surely be still well over one thousand souls.

Francis and I made our way back to the First Class Dining Room and here we were met by a strange sight. There were groups of steerage passengers who had stopped. They were gasping and talking in astonishment as they looked around at the splendour and opulence they had never seen before. The tables laid up with china, crystal, and fresh flowers, the chandeliers glowing, all looked so normal as if at any moment a waiter would arrive and shoo them out of the room. To these poor people, the sight of all this splendour must have been like a dream or fairy story come true. I remembered the first time that I had seen this room while with Francis on the tour of the ship. It seemed such a long time ago now. The delusion was suddenly shattered as a trolley at the far end of the room started to move and crashed into a table with a resounding crash. We felt a distinct tilt as *Titanic* settled farther into the sea.

We all made our way up to the Boat Deck again, emerging into the cold, dark night just as another distress rocket soared overhead. It was like being a spectator of a scene of some macabre play—the liner lay still and it was comparatively quiet on this part of the deck. Most of the boats had already gone, I noticed. The steerage passengers, who had gone ahead of us, were now on their knees, praying for deliverance.

I watched and saw there was no great urgency in launching the boats. And in fact several were being lowered that were not even full, which seemed a tragedy, as sooner or later it would be increasingly obvious that the boats were not going to be enough for all those still left on board. Many did not believe *Titanic* was doomed. They still believed it was not possible for such a gigantic ship to flounder. Others felt that rescue ships would arrive before dawn to take those left on board, so there was little point in their minds to sitting in a freezing cold lifeboat on the sea, when this would be totally unnecessary.

Francis and I toured the deck, and we stopped every

now and then to help the remaining crew assist people into the boats; many of the women were not too keen on leaving the warmth and comfort of the liner for the open sea.

The band had now donned life jackets, had moved up the Boat Deck, and positioned themselves at the entrance to the Grand Staircase. People were milling about, a scene of great tragedy. I even saw Captain Smith briefly, and he put his hand up to me in a kind of farewell salute. He had aged many years in those last few hours, and I wondered if I would ever see him again. The band kept on playing, keeping up people's morale with the lively ragtime tunes.

Francis and I decided to have one last tour before looking for a way to leave *Titanic*. We both knew without any doubt that she had little time left to live. It was strange at this time—I did not feel afraid of dying, or of the danger in jumping that seventy feet into the dark water below. I had a feeling of calm and a sort of inner peace, and I knew we had other responsibilities to attend to before we left. I was sad to leave *Titanic*. I had come to love this great ship over the last few days and felt my fate was mixed in with hers. I felt sad she would soon have to leave us for a watery grave two miles below, an environment and a fate she was never designed for.

The staterooms below were silent and the doors stood open. Trunks and discarded clothes littered the floor. The long companionways were quiet and silent now. Most of the passengers had found their way to the upper decks. A few had remained below, or in the warmth of the gymnasium or lounge. I saw a group of men playing cards as if it was just another ordinary evening on board. Francis asked if they were going topside, but they said they were fine. He did try again by asking them to put on their life jackets, but they just said goodnight to us both and continued playing.

I could not hold back the tears. I had come to feel for *Ti-*

tanic very much, and her impending loss affected me a great deal. She was such a beautiful grand ship, a place of laughter and pleasure, now doomed to disappear below the waves. I felt foolish and wiped my eyes. I looked at Francis to see if he had noticed and saw his eyes red also.

He turned to me then and said, "Don't worry, Edward. We will see this through together. We will have to go back to the deck soon. I don't think she has very long left to live."

As we passed the Radio Room, we stopped for a moment to listen to the faint blip-blip of the Morse key. Francis translated for me so that I could understand.

"C.Q.D., C.Q.D. (The call sign of *Titanic*), S.O.S., C.Q.D., S.O.S. Come at once, we have struck an iceberg. C.Q.D., O.M. (It's a C.Q.D., old man). Position 41 degrees North, 50 degrees 14 West, C.Q.D., S.O.S."

I asked Francis what the S.O.S. meant and he told me it was the new international call sign meaning, "Save Our Souls"; and for the second time that night, a cold shiver passed down my spine. The radio operator saw us standing there and said, "Don't worry, lads. The *Carpathia* has received our call and is heading our way at full speed. She is only fifty-eight miles away."

We left the Radio Room and continued to the deck. I asked Francis how long it would take the *Carpathia* to reach us, to which he replied that in his estimation from four to six hours. Neither of us spoke at that moment, as we knew she would be too late.

As we came again on the Boat Deck, we saw the last of the rockets reach into the clear sky. Francis pointed to a light on the horizon. It was another ship, which *Titanic* had been trying to contact for some time, but they had taken no notice, or the radio operator was asleep, or did not believe we were in any trouble, but surely if they had a lookout, they would have seen the rockets and known what they meant.

Francis said he wished he had a cannon, so he could wake them up. If they came alongside, everyone could be saved.

The last boats were leaving now. The davits hung limp and forlorn. There were few crew left to man the boats. One crew member was to man each boat, having some knowledge of seamanship, enough at least to be able to steer the boats away from the side of the great liner, and to get them away from the side in case she caused a great whirlpool and suction when she finally sank.

We watched the scene in fascination. As there was some confusion at the number 10 lifeboat, we went over to see if we could help in any way. The problem was that owing to the slant of *Titanic*, passengers were having to jump the two feet from the side of the ship into the boat, and many of the women were not too keen on this. We helped people step over and then helped to lower the boat to the water. It was difficult to keep her level to prevent her occupants from falling out.

At number 13 there was also confusion. One of the woman passengers refused to get in, saying it was an unlucky number, but a crew member just picked her up, and the woman found herself dumped unceremoniously on the bottom of the boat, shouting that there were men hiding under the seats, but we had little time to check the boat and she was lowered into the water. As she hit the water, she was suddenly caught in the wash of the condenser exhaust, which had the effect of carrying her very fast aft, directly under the place where number 15 would shortly be lowered. We noticed the impending tragedy and shouted, but number 15 continued to descend. Then I saw a stoker spring into the stern of Number 13 and quickly cut the falls that held her. She floated clear just as 15 struck the water.

All around us we saw acts of courage. Francis pointed to the huge frame of the first officer, Wilde, who was working like a madman to get the last few boats lowered safely, doing all he could to avert panic and maintain order and discipline with both passengers and crew. James Moody was there also. He saw us and gave us a friendly wave. Their work was invaluable at this stage, as most of the other seamen had already left the ship, and there were fewer and fewer men left to keep control and discipline; but all was calm, with no sign of any panic.

About 1:30 A.M., we saw Captain Smith heading for the radio cabin. We joined him. He spoke hardly a word, but put his arm around my shoulder and asked why I was still on board. I did not need to reply, as for me, like him, this was my ship, something very special, so special that we might even share her fate together.

As we entered the Radio Room, the captain reported that the engine room was flooded, so the dynamos would not be working for very much longer and they would lose power for the radio. The operators could now leave their posts and try to save themselves. He shook their hands, and Phillips passed the news on to *Carpathia* while Bride informed the *Baltic* that *Titanic* had been in a collision and was sinking fast.

Bride now moved to pick up his lifebelt, while Phillips picked up the signal from *Olympic,* the sister ship of *Titanic* and sent another appeal for help: "We are in collision with berg. Sinking. Head down. 41 degrees 46 North, 0 degrees 14 West. Come as soon as you can." As the message was being tapped, Bride strapped the lifebelt on his back. "Captain says get your boats ready. What is your position?"

The *Olympic* replied, "It's 40 degrees 52 North, 61 degrees 18 West. Are you steering southerly to meet us?"

Captain Smith paled as he digested this last message. Clearly the captain of the sister ship had no idea of the real danger that they were in.

Not long after this, the captain told the operators to leave. "Men, you have done your full duty. You can do no more. Abandon your cabin. It's every man for himself. Look out for yourselves. I release you. That's the way of it at this kind of time. Every man for himself!"

We now accompanied the captain back to the deck. He left us with the warning that *Titanic* had little time left to live and we were to see to our own safety. He walked towards the bridge, shoulders hunched, a broken man.

Back on the Boat Deck we found all the lifeboats had gone. We helped the crew to release the two inflatables, the Englehardt collapsible, and prepared them for launching. Captain Smith appeared, and I saw him cross the deck to pick up a little girl who was crying and calling for her mother. Both had tears in their eyes. He turned away and that was the final time I saw Captain Smith.

Francis and I now dived from the fore part of the bridge. As we hit the ice cold water, I gasped as I went down. My limbs went numb with the cold, and I felt my eyes start to close. I began to sink. Then miraculously I was being lifted and soon dumped into the bottom of a boat, with Francis close behind. We were being rowed away from *Titanic*, and I watched her final moments with incredible horror and fascination.

I saw a group of firemen and stokers come onto the sloping deck. They dived straight into the water. I looked around for Bill, but I saw no sign. I knew he would be the last to leave and probably was still deep inside *Titanic*, keeping the lights burning for as long as he could.

Then as Francis put his arms around my shoulders and we both shivered with the wet and the bitter cold, we watched her final moments as the water rushed up the deck and people scrambled for the highest point aft, hoping to leave death until the final moment.

The orchestra had just been playing the haunting tune "Autumn" before *Titanic* lifted high in the air. In the boats we were all silent, tears filling our eyes, tears for those still on board, tears for those who were parted from loved ones, and tears in her final moments for the greatest liner ever built.

Slowly, as we watched, ever so slowly, her stern lifted clear of the water and I saw her bright propellers glinting in the moonlight. She stood on end for a few moments, as if waiting for something, as if she wanted to say a final prayer to the world that she had known for such a short time; the lights still blazed even below the water. They glowed a strange eerie glow; the sound reached us of the boilers breaking free and sweeping through the bow. Next, slowly at first, then with increasing speed, she stood almost perpendicular, and there was a rending scream as she broke in two, then slipped silently below the waves.

I looked in fascination and great sadness. She had disappeared. There was no giant whirlpool, as everyone had expected, no great suction dragging everything down. To me it was as if the world stood still for a moment, then the sounds that I shall never forget for the rest of my life reached me. The cries for help in the water, women, men, and children clinging to bits of flotsam in the freezing unmerciful waters. Before the cold took hold of them, they passed into a sleep from which they would never wake. The worst sounds were of those who were drowning, the spluttering, the gasping for breath, and those in the final throes of drowning.

Nine
Rescue by the *Carpathia*

Above the surface of the water lay a grey vapour, almost like swirling smoke, which was extremely cold. Gradually the groans and calls for aid died away, leaving an uncanny silence behind. We saw many of the lifeboats not filled to capacity, and I could not comprehend why they had not gone back for those still in the water.

From what we saw at that time, there was only one real attempt to save life, and that was made by Lowe, the fifth officer in boat number 14; in fact it was his boat that had taken us in and so saved our lives. We were transferred to another boat soon after, which was not so full.

Our boat managed to pick up a few of those still alive; but many were frozen and had died of hypothermia when we came alongside. Others, those barely alive, were dragged on board. The night was clear and silent, but very cold indeed as we all huddled together in the boat waiting for dawn to break.

At last the sky began to lighten and the sea became more choppy. Most of us in the boat were half asleep and no one spoke. I looked around and saw that some of the lifeboats had been tied together, to prevent them drifting too far from each other. In still another, there appeared to be only women and children, with no men, not even a crew member. One of the ladies was rowing with great gusto, encouraging others to take her lead and row to keep warm. Some boats were only half full, others dangerously full, almost awash with water, and there was also an upturned collapsible. I could see several men and an officer standing on the top, trying to keep their balance. Others clung desperately to the side in the water.

As the sky lightened with the approaching dawn, *Carpathia* came into sight. We all cheered and started to row towards her. As we came alongside, one of the officers looked down and asked, "Where is *Titanic?*"

"Gone!" was the reply. "She sank at 2:20 A.M."

There was then silence from the officer. There was nothing else to say. It was then 4:20 A.M. He then spoke again. "Were there many people still on board when she sank?"

"Hundreds and hundreds, perhaps more than a thousand!" one passenger shouted back.

At this the full effect took place as the passengers lining the side of *Carpathia* gasped at the terrible tragedy that had taken place, seeing just a few pathetic drifting boats—all that was left of the finest and most luxurious liner ever built.

We were taken on board, some climbed rope ladders, others, including the children, were lifted aboard in huge nets, used in port for loading cargo. Then we were taken for warm clothes and drinks. The passengers of the *Carpathia* wept openly at the sight of so much loss and tragedy, women and children desperately searching for their loved ones whom they hoped had been placed in other boats or picked up. Most would be disappointed, and as this tragic fact dawned, they began to weep.

Great kindness and sacrifice were being shown on all sides, with cabins being given up or shared. Clothes and blankets were handed out, with much needed words of comfort.

As many went below to the warmth of the public lounges, Francis and I stayed to watch the lifeboats being off loaded. *Carpathia* now searched for any debris of *Titanic*, but little was found and few bodies. No one in the water was still alive.

As the last few passengers came aboard, and we joined the remnant for coffee and food, we were shivering with the cold. One woman came over, kissed me on the cheek, and shook Francis's hand. I felt really embarrassed. She was one of the people whom we had picked up out of the water, and she was very grateful. Indeed we had saved her life.

Then a hand rested on my shoulder and I turned to find the smiling face of Howard, who hugged me with tears in his eyes. He took me over to see his parents, who were sipping cups of steaming coffee. They were overjoyed to see me again and told me how worried they had been when they found I had left the lifeboat when on *Titanic*. They told of the terrible job they had of restraining Howard who wanted to join me. It was only the lowering of the boat that prevented his leaving it also. When they asked why I had done it, I made some feeble excuse about leaving a photograph of my mother in the cabin, and needing to go back for it. I don't know if they believed me or not, but I felt I had told the white lie convincingly, as they did not question me any more.

As we chatted, we felt *Carpathia* come alive under our feet as the engines were restarted. We went back on deck to look at where *Titanic* had last been. The *Carpathia* passed over the site where she had been a few times looking for any life, but there was only flotsam and debris. The bright stars had faded and the eastern horizon was luminous with the new day. In the distance it was possible to see the outline of ice, and every now and then, a tower of ice, as an iceberg stuck its head from the dark waters. I wondered which one had collided with *Titanic* to inflict that fatal blow.

In the evening, I saw Francis, who had been questioning the crew. Apparently we were on radio silence until we reached New York, and we were steaming now at full speed. The *Californian* had steered for the last known position of *Titanic*. She had been asked to look for and pick up any bodies. She had radioed later that she had not found any bodies and was resuming her journey. This surprised us, for there were so many in the water when *Titanic* sank. They would have been buoyed up by their life jackets anyway, but perhaps that had drifted away in the currents. Later we discovered that the cable-laying ship *Mackay-Bennet* had picked up at least two hundred bodies. It was said that for many weeks after the sinking, bodies and wreckage were being found. Many told that they gave the site of the tragedy a wide berth. It was supposedly haunted, and crew and passengers had heard the cries and the calls for help from the dead.

Ten

New York

On April 18th, *Carpathia* entered New York harbour. There was a faint mist over the waters of the harbour, the skyscrapers looked as if they were suspended in space. We passed the Statue of Liberty and tears came into my eyes. We should have come in triumph on the magnificent *Titanic*, but arrived a pathetic, meagre group, all that was left from that grand ship. The Statue, her arm reaching high into the air, held on the rim of her uplifted torch, people crowded for the first view of *Carpathia*. She had kept up her strict radio silence since we had been picked up, which appeared to me rather strange because so many people waited to see if their families and loved ones were among those who were saved. As we approached the Cunard pier, we were surrounded by small boats, not the flotilla of small boats that would have met us on our maiden voyage, but a flotilla of curious photographers and reporters, waiting to see who and what was left of *Titanic*.

Several boats came alongside, asking for news, but we had been instructed to say nothing until we had docked. Then I thought of that terrible night, and I knew I would have nightmares for a long time to come. I thought of Bill. I had his letter in my hand, and I wept silently for him. Francis stood by my side. He also said nothing and tears were falling down his cheek. He put his arm around my shoulder and we wept for all those who had been lost.

All of a sudden, there was a scuffle as a reporter tried to come on board so as to attempt to get exclusive rights to the story, but he had no chance to speak to us, being bundled off to be kept under lock and key until we finally docked.

Howard came over to join us. He shook my hand and said he would see me later. I was not too sure what he meant, but I said good-bye anyway.

I went now to the top deck. Francis had a report to make to the White Star Offices, and I needed time to be alone. I felt guilty for some reason. Perhaps it was because I was alive and so many were dead. I had nothing to lose, while so many of those people had lost so much. I knew Howard and his parents had been very kind to me, but I did not want anyone to feel any obligation towards me now. I would see the captain later, try to get some sort of work on a ship, and so work my passage back to England, although there was nothing there of a personal nature for me.

I watched the passengers disembark. Thousands had come to see us arrive, and the police were having quite a struggle keeping them behind the hastily erected barriers. The news reporters were dragging people by their shoulders, light bulbs flashing on their cameras as they all wanted news of the tragedy.

It was pathetic now to see the sorry remnants of *Titanic* leave the ship. There were no piles of trunks and mountains of luggage. Noticeable was the fact that there were so few children and men amongst the survivors. What children were there looked frightened by the attention and clung to their parents' or guardians' hands. Two-thirds of the Steerage passengers had drowned, and those who were left looked to have aged a great deal in the past few days.

The atmosphere was strange. It was good to arrive back

on land. There was great sadness and also elation at finding that a relative thought lost was now alive, but many more had not returned. Francis asked me if I would like to go back to England with him as soon as we could. He had a sister who lived on the south coast overlooking the sea, and I could go to a proper school. I was glad he had offered and I knew he meant it, but he would be away most of the time, as I knew it would not be long before he found another job on a liner, perhaps even the *Olympic*. I wanted really to try to find a job on a ship and work my way up, the way he had.

Our chat was interrupted as we noticed some excitement on the deck below. We saw an excited man rush on board. Francis told me it was Guglielmo Marconi, the man who had invented the wireless, and so made it possible for *Titanic* to radio for help from the middle of the ocean. Many of us owed our lives to him, for being stuck in a lifeboat more than eight hundred miles from shore, in those freezing North Atlantic conditions, we would have had little chance to survive.

Most of the passengers had by now disembarked, and the few pathetic *Titanic* boats were being off loaded onto the quay. Francis and I made our way past the radio office where Marconi was talking to Bride. His greatest hope was that before long all ships would have radios, which could be manned twenty-four hours a day.

We both sat down in the quiet dining room and had a grand lunch. Then Francis asked if I would like to go on a tour of the city. He would enjoy showing me the sights, and perhaps it would help to take our minds off the terrible events of the past few days.

Before we left the ship, the captain asked to see us and told Francis that he had indeed been offered a post on *Olympic*, which pleased him very much. He saw my disappointment and told me he would try to get me a job on the same ship if he could, but he would like me to go to college and learn seamanship properly, so that I could in time become an officer for the White Star Line. So we left the dining room after lunch and in better spirits made our way to the dock, which was quiet now after all the excitement of that morning.

New York really amazed me. Those towering buildings called skyscrapers almost reached into the clouds. We were both almost like children, excited by all the traffic and people rushing through the streets. We got on really well. It was very much like that first day we had met, only a few days before when he had first showed me *Titanic*.

We went to Central Park, an area of green woodland right in the centre of one of the largest cities in the world, and here we both had an enormous multicoloured ice cream. Afterwards, we went to the zoo and marvelled at the animals. I had been once in England, but only as a small child and could not remember very much about it. Over a cold drink, Francis handed me a long parcel in brown paper. It was a present, he told me, he had managed to buy while I was busy buying yet another ice cream. I was very excited and opened it immediately. Inside was the most wonderful model I had ever seen—it was perfect in every detail, and in gold letters painted on the prow was the name RMS *Titanic*. Francis told me that he had seen Bill a short time before the end of the ship, and he had asked him to buy the model for me. At this I felt really sad, but also pleased. It was the best present I had ever received.

In the late afternoon, we took in a movie, which was what the Americans called a film. I had never seen the moving pictures before and enjoyed it very much indeed. It was so funny that I felt quite sick when I came out.

On emerging again onto the streets, we found it was now dark. The sight was overpowering, as the City of New

York was lit up with massive neon signs, advertising all sorts of products from Coca-Cola to ice cream. The noise of the traffic was deafening, the cars and buses rushing and filling the streets. I had never imagined there were so many cars in the world. We walked for miles and stopped for a drink and a meal in one café before heading back for the dock.

Just as we turned back, Francis bought a paper and when he opened it, we both had quite a shock, for our faces stared at us from the main headlines: "Stowaway Rescues Survivors!" Francis read the article aloud. It went on to describe both Francis and me, how we had helped people off the ship, and stopped to pick up people from the icy waters. We were even more surprised when we got back onboard ship. There was a call for us. It was from the President of the United States in Washington. He invited us to the White House in two weeks time.

I was very excited and went to bed that night with a smile on my face. But as usual I woke after a few hours, with a now familiar nightmare of those upturned, pale faces in the ocean water crying for help, and the terrible sounds of gurgling panic as so many drowned, and the final awful picture of *Titanic* upended and the final plunge into the dark depths. I woke screaming and sweating freely, Francis came and put his arm around me to ease those terrible pictures from my mind. I slept again and when I awoke, it was daylight. The sun was streaming through the portholes into our cabin. The sounds of traffic and horns resounded from the city that never sleeps. I leaned over to see if the model was still safe. It was my prized possession.

After breakfast in the dining room, we were told there were reporters who wanted to talk to us. Furthermore, Howard's parents also wanted to speak to us. I saw them first, and they invited me to live with them. They told me they had a huge house overlooking the harbour, where I could see the great liners entering and leaving the habour. Howard also needed a good companion. Would I come?

I had a few minutes with Francis, who persuaded me it was a grand idea, and that he could visit anytime he was in New York, which would be at least once a week, if he was on *Olympic*. So I accepted with pleasure. Within a few minutes, I had found new parents and a new brother. I already had a good friend in Francis.

Just one more surprise greeted me at my new home, for as promised, the bedroom in the huge mansion that was to be mine was overlooking the harbour, where the liners could be seen entering and leaving New York Harbour. I could even see clearly the Statue of Liberty, and there by the side of the bed, in all its glory, was a brand new bicycle.